NOW IS *Your* TIME

It's Your Turn - It's Your Time

D'vora Power

Now Is Your Time
© 2015 D'vora Power

NOTICE OF RIGHTS
Manufactured in the United States of America. No part of this book may be reproduced, transmitted in any form or by any means—electronic, or mechanical—including photocopying and recording, or by any information storage or retrieval system, except as may be expressly permitted in writing by the publisher or author.

NOTICE OF LIABILITY
The information in this book is distributed on an "as is" basis, for informational purposes only, without warranty. While every precaution has been taken in the production of this book, neither the copyright owner nor the publisher shall have any liability to any person or entity with respect to any liability, loss, or damage caused or alleged to be caused directly or indirectly by the information contained in this book.

ISBN 13: 978-1-937660-51-2
ISBN 10: 1978660516
eBook ISBN: 978-1-937660-52-9

Published by:
Heritage Press Publications, LLC
PO Box 561
Collinsville, MS 39325

Cover design: Christine E. Dupre

Dedication

Dedicated to my loving husband, Joseph, my son, David, my daughter, Rachel, my grandchildren, and my great-grandchild.

TABLE OF CONTENTS

Chapter 1
The Beginning
1

Chapter 2
Dreams Really Do Come True
9

Chapter 3
The Valley of the Shadow of Death
15

Chapter 4
Homeward Bound
25

Chapter 5
Close Encounters with My Healer and Bodyguards
39

Chapter 6
My Turning Point
49

Chapter 7
This is Not the End...Only the Beginning
61

About the Author
67

Dreams Do Come True! It Can Happen to You!
69

Chapter 1

The Beginning

Now Is Your Time

I was born and I was raised.

Then I moved to Texas.

Of course, there's so much more to my story. If you hung out with me long enough, you would get to hear it all, but for this moment, we will not go into "it" here. Now is NOT the time for "that."

The story you are going to hear is about right now, because, now is the time for this!

Now Is The Time!

As I am a woman of great belief and prayer, may I offer a prayer as you read my story? Okay, good—I thought you'd agree.

Father, I pray for the one who is holding this book in their precious hands right now. I pray this story will not only bless their lives, but will add and multiply within their lives. May the words of my story bring them freedom to live in the now, in this present moment. Amen.

Let's begin a journey, you and me. Let's take a little trip and wander off for a while. Let's shut out the world; let's turn off all sound. Let's stop and get off the merry-go-round and just be.

Now Is Your Time

Being you is not only perfect, it is your purpose. You are awesome! Believe me, I know. Oh sure, there are some things you wish you could change about yourself, and there's time for that. Yet, being you is perfect in that no one is you *but you*. I know this, I can hear you thinking. But are you *you* all the time, or do you conform to whatever or whomever when a situation arises? Let's be honest.

For me, I have always conformed at the drop of a hat in order to be loved, accepted, and approved of. Did I just say that out loud? Yes, I did. Okay, no worries.

I have learned I am who I AM says I am. And so are you. You are beautiful, you are wonderful, and you are amazing. You were created by a holy, divine Creator, and when I look into your eyes, I see how beautiful He must be.

Let me share a story with you about my sister, Rose. Rose was always straightforward in that she always spoke her mind, she didn't mince words, and she really didn't care how you felt about it. She was real and the type who was in your face ,but in a calm, kind way. She had confidence that what she was telling you was truth—hers. I loved my sister Rose very much, especially for her no-nonsense ways. Rose was also my memory. If I had forgotten something from our past, she always remembered and in detail. She was amazing at remembering details, names, places, occurrences. I miss her, I ache for her. I miss her as my friend. "My Posie" is what Dad used to call her—"Rosie Posie." She was really something else.

In the middle of 2012, I received a call. It was one of those calls you never want to answer. My brother called to give me some horrible news—news that broke my heart and brought me to tears. My sister, Rose, had just been diagnosed with stage-four lung cancer. As he described in detail what the doctors had said, my heart sank deeper and deeper. This was not good, and her surviving this was going to take a miracle.

No miracle came for Rose.

On November 11, 2012, she took her final breath. Just like that, she was gone. I had promised her I would hold her hand until the end, and I did.

In quiet moments of reflection, as her only son sat closely by listening intently, she shared her regrets. "I thought I'd have more time," she said.

We always think this. My question is, why? We are not promised tomorrow. No, my precious friends, all we have is NOW. I capitalize that word as a shout-out, as a true statement, as a fact we all know so well.

Death comes.

We die.

Now Is Your Time

When it is our time, nothing can stop it. And so I begin this story with the reality that I am still here. I am still alive and kicking, and so are you. Why?

Why is a good question. It's one only you can answer, but a question that needs an answer nonetheless. The sooner you answer this question, the sooner you will BE YOU, the sooner YOU WILL DO what you came here to do, and the sooner YOU WILL HAVE what you want.

It seems like an easy task, but it's not. It takes effort, energy, and time.

You need time to think and that takes effort. You need the energy to persist until you have the answer. You need to give yourself time to explore and wonder, and time to question everything. You need to question yourself and your thoughts, and give yourself time to consider why you were created.

We know you are here for a purpose, but what is it? Only YOU have the answers.

Do you know? Do you want to know?

I mean isn't there more? There has to be!

At one time I believed I had the answers, but I had thought that before. So many times I had believed I knew the answers to why me, why do I exist, and what was my purpose for being. On and on the wondering continued, the questions came, and just as easily they went.

My life was just ebbing away, day by day. The numerous times of just going through the motions, existing, being this, and being that—for whom and why? I mean, I know I am not the only one who has gone through this process. Are you there now?

Then great! Let's begin again, shall we?

It's okay. Everything that has happened up to this point is all okay. It has to be. We can undo nothing. The choices we made, the decisions we believed at the time were the right ones and we realize now weren't—all these can serve a purpose in God's design and grand scheme. Nothing is ever wasted. Everything we have gone through has brought us right here to this very moment. Isn't it time to discover or uncover what it is about you that you need to know?

What is "it?"

What is your "it?"

Who are you?

Why are you?

Again, I assure you—you already know. You already have the answers! And that's the good news.

Now Is Your Time

Somehow, we have connected, and this book has found its way to you. I believe the book in your hands, right this minute, is by divine design. We have either joined forces to make a difference here on planet earth, or we were brought together for just a little while. For whatever the reason, for whatever purpose, I am happy we are here together now.

There's no time like the present! My message to you is this: It's Your Turn and It's Your Time!

Receive the gift of now!

Right now!

Chapter 2

Dreams Really Do Come True

Now Is Your Time

Now Is Your Time

Have you ever won an all-expense paid trip, ever?

Well, I did!

December 2013, I was going strong and working hard to make my dreams come true. The result was a cruise to Belize, Honduras, and Cozumel aboard Carnival Magic—all expenses paid!

It wasn't magic that got me aboard Magic—it was my time, my efforts and my energy. My energy began to decrease sorely two weekends before the trip. I wasn't listening to my body. I was too busy. Both weekends prior to boarding, I found myself with flu-like symptoms that had me collapsed in bed with the covers over my head.

Scott Pritchard, our senior marketing director, offered to come pray for me and I politely thanked him, but I didn't want him to go out of his way or be a bother. I have since apologized to him and have learned my lesson to never refuse prayer again. It's a lesson I will never forget.

On Sunday morning, December 15, 2013, I dragged myself out of bed, grabbed two pillows and a blanket and climbed into the back seat of Jojo and Jett's car (they were part of the group going on the cruise), and slept all the way to Galveston. Jett gave me something she had picked up at Whole Foods (some crystals I let it dissolve on my tongue) and like magic, I felt healed!

At least long enough to board the ship.

Once in the cabin, tennis shoes off and still in my jeans, I jumped into bed. I managed to go for dinner that night, but my appetite was disappearing. James, the CEO of the company, and Sarah, his wife, had made goodie bags for all the winners of the cruise, and so I tried some M & M peanuts. There was no taste at all to them; something wasn't right.

Monday, I asked Joseph (my husband) to put the "do not disturb" sign on the door. All day and all night I stayed in bed. Security knocked on our door that evening because I think the maid had come at her usual times, saw the sign, and reported us. Joseph told security I was tired and just wanted sleep and rest. The security guard went away with no questions asked.

Much later in the evening, we received another knock at the door. Wondering who this could possibly be, Joseph went to open the door. Our family was in the hall and began singing Christmas carols. They were hilarious! I laughed with joy at their sweetness and love, but I wanted to cry. I felt so bad physically, but also emotionally, because we were not enjoying the trip with them.

In order to not cause suspicion, Tuesday morning we got up and left the room. I was weak. I had to hold onto Joseph just to walk. We ran into Brett, Mark, and Cori (more people from our group) in the dining room. They expressed concern as we sat with them, and I think I said I was okay, but all I wanted to do was lay down. I thought I was going to pass out.

In order not to upset anyone, I went to dinner. There were twenty-five of us—a big group from the office who had won the trip, plus Sarah's family (our CEO's wife), and his in-laws. Everyone was enjoying the sea, the trip, the food, and the fun, yet were concerned for me. Everyone was praying for me to get well.

Wellness was not coming.

Wednesday and Thursday were the worst nights of our lives. We could not sleep. My cough had gotten so bad, I could not lie down. I could not sleep so I took showers and propped myself up on two pillows on the vanity table. By hunching over them, I managed to rest a little.

Thursday morning we went to down to medical and we were told it would cost $140 to see the doctor. I felt that was outrageous, so I bought a six dollar bottle of cough syrup that lasted two seconds because the bottle was so small.

Now Is Your Time

Joseph was upset, actually mad at God, "Why won't He heal you?" he questioned me. I didn't know and wondered myself, but I kept trying to calm him down, saying I'd be ok.

Nothing was okay.

Thursday night passed and midnight arrived. It was Friday, December 20, 2013. By the time that day got there, I felt my life had a dimmer switch on it and it was slowly being turned down to "off." I felt like everything was dimming, becoming dark...

Chapter 3

The Valley of the Shadow of Death

Now Is Your Time

My first thought was, *What's happening? This is weird.* Everything was dimming around me and a darkness seemed to be growing and settling around me. I felt my life seeping out of my body and I was getting weaker and weaker. Exhausted, I began to walk, pacing actually, around the cabin, trying to be quiet and not disturb what little rest or sleep Joseph may have gotten.

Something is happening, but what? I kept talking to myself, muttering. This had never happened to me before and I kept asking myself, *What is this?* Not only was I feeling a little scared, the words I heard in my head were Job's and Job's wife's words.

Wife: "Curse God and die!"

Job: "The Lord gives and the Lord takes. Blessed be the name of the Lord!"

Reality began to grip me, and I knew that I was dying. It was surreal. The darkness seemed to be settling like a real dark cloud upon me as I walked to Joseph's side of the bed. The space was small and I just stood there.

Joseph asked me what was wrong and I said, "I'm dying."

I said it like you would say hello, like a fact. He reacted by jumping up quickly. What was I talking about? How could this be happening? He got angry, mad! He was raising his voice to God.

"Why won't You help her?" I tried to calm him down. Why, why, why was right. We didn't understand.

Have you ever found yourself in a strange place? You don't know how you got there and you don't know how to leave. We were there. Now what?

And "Now what?" is the perfect question to ask at a time like that. For some of us, when we don't know what to do, we do nothing—which I believe is wisdom.

I prayed, and I mean seriously prayed, pleading for my life. But since childhood, I have always ended my prayers with, "Not my will, but Yours be done, Father." Isn't that how Yeshua taught us?

I thought about Job. He had lost everything in one day! I could understand how distraught his wife felt. I could only imagine how a parent would feel losing their children. Job lost all his kids in one day! All of them!

I had lost nothing. I was on a seven-day cruise I had won and was with my family, friends and associates. This was an award trip; we had worked hard to win this. My only intention was to have a blast at sea for seven days. I had never been to Belize and was supercharged that I would get to see it first hand.

Little did I know my lungs had decided not this time, not this trip.

In fact, maybe never!

I preach constantly that we should listen to our bodies, and I knew something wasn't right. Ask anyone I know and they'll tell you it is one of my personal mantras. And I was listening to my own body, but I could not figure out exactly what it was saying except "something" was NOT right. All I could do was pray, pray, pray!

How do you explain or understand the valley of the shadow of death? I can't. All I can say to explain it was that it was getting dark.

I began to pray to the Father, going through the stages of grief in rapid succession.

Shock, denial, anger, bargaining, depression, and acceptance. I was barreling through these like a hurricane, my heart whirling as if in a tornado.

And I was in the whirlwind…of death. Inside me, everything was at a fever pitch and I was right at the edge. I will never forget it.

Still, out of sheer desperation I begged and pleaded. "Really, Father, now? You want me now? I am only sixty-one. I have never had any major illness. If it is Your will for me to come home, You know I want Your will, but now? I mean, I would really like to stay. I have a great-grandson being born in March. I don't want to miss Bryce! I don't want to miss ANYTHING! Nevertheless, Thy will be done."

And I kept hearing my spirit repeating that phrase..."Thy will be done."

It was dark...spiritually. I was scared, yet somehow not afraid or fearful. I had a peace, like a cozy warm blanket enveloping me. It made no sense but that's where I was at emotionally.

"I don't care how much it costs, you are going to see the doctor as soon as medical opens." Joseph was almost screaming. I think I dialed the medic department on the cabin phone and got no answer. It rang and rang and rang and still, no answer.

But Joseph was adamant—he didn't care if it cost $1000. I was going to the doctor!

Weak, I stumbled about the cabin, taking another shower to help myself feel better. The coughing would not cease. There was no comfortable position to place myself in with this pain in my chest except the hands of the Father.

Joseph was beside himself with fear, anger, and confusion. It was taking every ounce of my strength to keep him calm.

As soon as the medical office opened at 8:00 a.m., we were down there. The doctor on call ran his assessment as normal, and then took a chest x-ray. He could not believe his eyes. He asked us to join him in a closet-size hall so he could show us a normal x-ray with a little pneumonia. He wanted to compare it to my x-ray.

He was quite concerned and said I needed to get to the emergency room as soon as possible. My lungs were infiltrated. They were a solid white mass. There were no shadows and no dark lobes could be seen. There was nothing, as if my lungs no longer existed. He said, "Mrs. Fischer, I don't know how you're still alive."

He placed me on oxygen, gave me something for my nerves, and called for an ambulance. We were docked in Cozumel for the day and by then, it was almost 1:30 p.m. We had been five and a half hours in medical.

He placed me in a compact, hospital-like room in a tiny bed made for a child. There were two like it, both pushed up against the wall. There was a porthole I could see out of. I laid down and rested for the first time in forty-eight hours. I felt safe in the belly of the ship. In and out of sleep, I prayed. As the sun beamed into the room, and with oxygen flowing, I felt light and LIGHT; the darkness was at bay.

Recently, my nephew, James, shared with me a Jim Rohn observation (I love Jim, may he rest in peace).

James said, "When the light is turned on, how far away is the darkness?"

"As far as the light goes?" I replied.

James said, "Yes, where light ends, darkness begins. It's always ready to come back to the place it has been given. It's always waiting to return." It made sense to me, and in Mexico, that's exactly what happened.

The first remedy was with oxygen, and my brain was being revived. And that equals more LIGHT and less darkness! My O2 saturation had been decreasing in those early hours, and when that darkness descended upon me, it was very real. I was really dying from lack of oxygen, thus the shadow of the Valley of death was indeed real!

Let me digress just a minute—we're told in real-life situations to place the mask over ourselves first. Why? We know the answer, which goes back to the truth that you have the answers for you, for your life. You already know what you must do. It's a matter of *will* you do what you need to do?

It's time for some:

- Realization
- Revelation
- Re-firing!

It's time for a resurrection of you—the real YOU!

It's time for us to realize who we are, It's time to reveal who we are and it's time to get FIRED up about it!

Let's get back on the boat! Joseph was sent up to pack all our stuff and guest services was able to help speed the process. From there, the pace of things picked up.

Do you sense an urgency within? Does it feel like life is speeding up?

Now Is Your Time

Does it feel like it's too late for you?

Are you hearing the question WHY more?

GOOD! GREAT! Because... NOW is the time!

It's your turn, and it's your time! All we have is now—tomorrow may be too late!

Today is what matters...

All we have is today...and that's all we are promised!

CHAPTER 4

Homeward Bound

Now Is Your Time

Now Is Your Time

Sometimes, we have to almost die in order to LIVE!

The light (my life) was going out like a candle that gets to the end of the wick. Darkness was seeking to take over, because that's what darkness does. I didn't know how sick I was, and I had no history of anything like this before. I was normally healthy.

I wasn't struggling to breathe, but inside, in my lungs, a virus, a fungus—something—had entered and a chain of reactions had begun. That "something" was going to run its course. My lungs were sick and in distress, and my body was compensating as best it could. I had no control of what was happening.

My life was indeed hanging in the balance.

In my late twenties, I had been choked to the point that everything went black, and I knew I was being strangled. All I could do after fighting to get free was simply just let go. When I did, my attacker let go and I slumped up against a wall and slid to the floor. I didn't pass out completely, but I came close. I was almost killed that day, but wasn't.

Have you ever tasted death? Have you ever been in a place so dark you thought you were going to die? Then you can relate to what I am saying. I think we can experience many kinds of near-death experiences and be fully alive.

Now Is Your Time

We are such powerful, beautiful intricate creatures. We are spirit, soul, body, and mind. We can have spiritual, emotional, mental, and physical close encounters with death. These wounds can run so deeply that we may suppress even the memory of them without even being aware of it. Yet, we know something isn't quite right. We feel stalled, stuck. We may even wrestle with our sanity when it gets very dark.

My life wasn't flashing before my eyes. It seemed all was well now that I had oxygen on board and medicine to reduce the anxiety of it all. Once we were shown the x-ray and told what was happening, we weren't happy with the news, but I was still alive. That was good news, and where there is life, there is hope.

For Rose, my sister, her news came too late. It was Sunday, November 5, 2012, and she was back in the hospital again. She had called me by accident. She couldn't breathe and she was trying to call her daughter, Jessica, who had stepped out to get a cup of coffee.

She was gasping for air and filled with anxiety.

"Jessica?" she asked.

"No, babe, this is Deb."

"I can't breathe!! Pray for me," she pleaded in desperation. The fear in her voice scared me and I began to pray, telling her to breathe slower.

"Push the call light! Call the nurse" I said. She did, and immediately, the nurse answered. Within seconds, I could hear her voice at my sister's bedside.

Rose's last words to me, through very labored breaths, were, "I love you. Goodbye." We were in Tennessee. We packed and drove straight through all night and by the time we got to the hospital, she was on the ventilator and in intensive care.

It was the last week of her life. On November 11, 2012, she breathed her last. My heart broke. My sister, my friend, was gone.

Breathe...

Live...

Dream…

Believe…

Begin, again…

Today.

Now Is Your Time

Choose life.

I had to almost die in order to know I wanted to live!

The paramedics arrived. They came in and got me on the gurney as my husband met us at the door with our luggage. It was perfect timing. As we reached the dock walkway, other passengers were coming back from their excursions of the day. I got a lot of stares. Some were looks of fear, while others were looks of compassion.

By then it was 2:00 p.m. I kept praying we would see someone we knew, a family member, a friend, but none of them knew what was taking place. And we wouldn't be back in time for the ship's departure as it was leaving at 4:30 p.m. We stayed calm, but we were anxious inside.

However, our prayers were answered, and perfect timing. Joseph spotted some of our group (Brett at 6'6" was easy to see!). James, Brett, Tony, and Bode just happened to be coming back to the ship from shore. We were able to tell them what was happening. We had no choice.

I could hear them talking outside the ambulance. Within seconds, both back doors flew open and there they stood. Bode, five-years-old, climbed up into the cab. He stood on the bumper to get a better look.

James asked if I was okay (as he was handing me his credit card), and if I needed anything. I thanked him, but said no. He asked if I was going to be all right as we looked into each other's eyes. I assured him I was. Our connection has always been strong.

Bode said, "We love you, DD" and I told him I loved him too. We gave each other words of love and we said our goodbyes. They closed the doors and off we went.

Knowing we were going to be left in Mexico didn't bring me or my husband comfort. But here we were, having no clue as to how we would get home or what might happen next.

The ride was short and the hospital was small. Upon arrival, I was wheeled into an emergency room stall. The curtain did not reach both sides of the doorway. A young nurse who only spoke her language came in and took my vital signs, then left. We tried to communicate, but with little success. A doctor came after a while, and he did speak English. He asked a lot of questions, then left.

A man came to speak to Joseph. He wanted our passports and eighty-six American dollars. Joseph came in and asked if we should give them to him. I guessed we had to. The man promised to get us past security and that he'd get us our passports back. It would take a while, he said, but he'd meet us at the airport (which he did).

Another man came and asked for $3000. He said we had to pay them $3000 before we could be released. Joseph told him we didn't have $3000. The man suggested maybe we had family that could wire the money, but Joseph said he didn't think so.

The hospital assigned a liaison for us. His name was Alejandro and he quickly placed us in contact with the air evacuation company Air Medical, a twenty-four-hour dispatch service out of San Antonio, Texas.

My husband, Alejandro, and Zach from Air Medical began the process of arranging for us to be flown out of Mexico by 9:00 p.m. that evening, December 20.

We overheard snatches of conversation that they needed to evac me out so I would not die in Mexico. It was intense.

The young nurse returned and began to prepare me to go into another room. She wheeled me, with Joseph's help, to an isolation room and gave us a menu. I chose "sandwich" and "pasta." the only two words I could read and point to.

She returned later with a lettuce sandwich for Joseph and some pasta for me. I took a bite or two, but had no sense of taste or desire for food. I hadn't eaten all day. There was nothing to drink on the dinner tray, but later we were given water as we had requested. I was very uncomfortable. There was no pillow on the bed. My only hope and prayer was that Air Medical was on their way.

My husband was told several times that if we could not come up with $3000, we would not be permitted to leave the hospital. For hours before Air Medical got there (and for almost two hours after they got there), my husband was in one administration office or another, pretty much begging for his wife's body to be released. All this time my lungs worsening.

It was unbelievable! It felt like we were being held for ransom...almost like a hostage situation. We had given them our BCBS insurance card—what more did they want? (BCBS paid the hospital in full.)

At 9:00 p.m. the "Calvary" arrived (Air Medical). They quickly assessed me, began administering the proper air flow, hung IV fluids and some IV relaxing meds, and I was finally able to relax.

For two hours, from 9:00 p.m. until 11:00 p.m., Randal and James from Air Medical watched over me. When we offered up our Discover card to the hospital, the charges suddenly jumped to $5000! My husband was furious! He told them we'd pay them $3000 and in return, they would have to give us an itemized bill for the charges. I believe they told him they couldn't, for whatever reasons.

Finally we were able to leave! The man who had our passports was there at the airport waiting, and got us cleared to leave. I was feeling much safer and content knowing I was headed home toAmerica! Joseph was too. He could relax, sit back, and get some much needed sleep.

It had been an experience, but it was far from over.

Our pilot met us outside the Learjet. He greeted me, introduced himself, and promised he'd get us home safely. I believed him. He assisted the crew getting me into the plane. The plane was super cool and it was tiny. I felt like a princess. I thought, All this for me?

The flight was two hours and fifty minutes, I heard them say. It seemed to go pretty fast. James and Randall made sure I was comfortable at all times, and my husband as well.

Again, it was an amazing flight. James kept promising he'd save some cookies for his wife that Randall's mom had made, but we both knew that James wasn't going to stop eating until that goody bag was empty (he did try a few times).

James and Randal were professional, fast, and their sense of humor calmed not only my nerves, but also my precious husband's fearful heart that he was losing his wife.

It was amazing to watch as the observant patient.

They kept me laughing. I was no longer in pain. I felt really good. My body was being oxygenated, my nerves were bathed in medicine, and two awesome earth angels, James and Randal, kept a very close eye on all my vitals—writing, recording, and checking this and that. I drifted off and on as we flew. I lay there counting my blessings, even though my lungs wanted to say goodbye. I had such serene peace that my Father above was in control, and He, being my Healer, was holding me tight.

It was an amazing experience! I highly recommend any of these men who gave such great care and service to me that night and strongly encourage raises or bonuses, because in my eyes, they went above and beyond. They are our heroes!

We arrived in San Antonio, Texas. It was raining, misting, and we had just gone through a storm. Our pilot and copilot were terrific!

Out on the tarmac, a security baggage officer stood in the misting rain. It was a chilly morning. He swiftly checked the bags and told Joseph that he'd been praying for me. Joseph thanked him and the man wished us well.

I was covered with a white sheet up to my neck, so my face was exposed to the mist. On my back, I saw the sheets of rain coming down in perfect raindrops as the light from the tarmac lamps illuminated it all. It was beautiful. I love rain, especially the misting kind. Joseph loves soft rain, which is a little heavier.

We arrived at the Methodist Texsan Hospital and I was brought to the second floor. It was now Saturday, December 21, 2013 about 3:30 a.m. James and Randal gave report as the new nurse got me all hooked up to her monitors.

Randal and James prepared to leave. We hugged their necks and thanked them for everything. We believe they helped save my life.

A white haired doctor came in next. He was the on-call emergency room doctor for the day. He listened to my lungs, spoke briefly to us and left. He ordered me into ICU where I spent my next ten days.

On his morning rounds, he called Joseph out of my room to show him the x-ray again. He told Joseph that, after admitting me into the hospital with pneumonia, he went home but couldn't sleep. He said he prayed for me because he thought I would not make it. He thought by the time he got there for rounds, I'd be dead.

I wasn't.

The doctor used the word "miracle."

Joseph was so scared, he seemed lost. I didn't like the look on his face, but after thirty years, I knew he was just afraid. However, with everything going on, this did not help my husband's fear decrease. My husband shared all this days later with me when I was more awake.

Another doctor came into the room, asking me if I had a living will and did I want every measure taken to save my life. I remember saying "Yes." He explained that they might have to place me on ventilation and put an nasal-gastric tube in to feed me to keep me alive.

It all sounded like a nightmare to me! How could this be happening? How could I be so sick, so near death? But it was real.

I remember saying to this young doctor, "I don't want to be on a vent," and his response was very matter of fact. "Well, it's like this—if we don't, you may die."

Now Is Your Time

I realized I was in trouble if they were going to have to put me into a drug-induced coma. I agreed that, in order to keep me alive, whatever it took, they needed to do. I was willing, but it really scared me. I think that was the moment I realized I was in some serious trouble.

However, peace was still mine.

Every nurse, doctor, respiratory person, nursing assistant, housekeeping, dietary, x-ray tech, CT person—everyone seemed to be on Team Deb's team and everyone appeared to be angels. I do not know exactly when, but my husband began writing down everyone's name. He said, "Well, it's something you would do." I am so grateful he wrote the list of everyone who helped save my life.

Now, the challenge was on! It was fight or die!

My story with this message is an "I dare you" challenge. I dare you to BE you! I dare you to DO the things you love only and what makes you happy! I dare you to BE Happy, NOW!

I DARE you to love and be loved!

Now, today, and everyday for the rest of your life!

I double dare you!!

Chapter 5

Close Encounters With My Healer and Bodyguards

Now Is Your Time

I don't remember the exact night, but I did see past the "veil" into the spiritual realm. It was awesome, yet very sobering.

I believe it was the second or third night I spent in ICU. They had placed a CPAP machine on me to help me breathe. I wasn't happy about this, but it was better then being ventilated. For some reason I have a small case of claustrophobia and, I don't like feeling smothered. None of us do.

So, CPAP was challenging for me. Yet, it was keeping me alive.

I became my own coach. I had to stop myself from freaking out. I remember talking to myself, calmly saying, "Its okay, you can do this. You have to do this. It's going to be okay."

I would actually remove the mask to help myself cope. But then the device would beep to alarm the staff it was off so, then I'd place it back on so the beeping would stop. Of course, each time I did that my O_2 saturation would drop, which was not good.

I felt very vulnerable and weak, yet determined to beat this thing. I was going to get through this somehow, some way.

Now Is Your Time

I was struggling. I did not like the CPAP at all. I was having trouble relaxing or sleeping. The mask and machine were irritating to me. I tried to relax, I tried all my tricks, and nothing seemed to be working. My praying increased, and I knew many were praying for me. I was very grateful. My son, David, and Rachel, my daughter, called several times a day, both wanting to come to Texas to be with me.

David lived in Colorado and Rachel lived in Louisiana. Both had responsibilities and families they were caring for, so I told them not to come, that I'd be okay. I knew it was an expense they couldn't afford, and I didn't want them to feel more stressed than they already were.

Every time I closed my eyes that night, something very strange would happen. Something I had never felt nor have felt since. Every time I closed my eyes, I would feel hands touching my body.

A pair of hands would touch me and startle me. I would open my eyes, but no one was there. At first I really didn't pay too much attention to it because I was going in and out of sleep. *Maybe I'm just dreaming*, I thought, and I'd go back to sleep, only to be awakened again by the hands!

Okay, I thought, surely this time the RN, or CNT, or the respiratory tech was here to give me a treatment, but NO ONE was there. I could see Joseph was asleep. He wasn't touching me. I began to wonder if I was hallucinating!

It was real. It was very real.

This happened again and again, and my praying intensified. Lay your hands right now, both hands, on yourself somewhere. Feel that? That's what I was feeling. But notice I said a "pair" of hands. So to really feel what I am describing, you need to feel another pair of hands, not yours, touching you as you try to sleep. Then you will know exactly what I felt. Then imagine when you feel these hands and open your eyes, no one's there.

Has anyone, ever placed their hands on you at night? Usually, if I place my hands on my husband during the night, especially if I am standing next to the bed, he wakes up startled. His response is usually, "What's wrong?"

The hands were now coming every time I closed my eyes.

Upon awakening again, what I saw this time was amazing! I saw three angels standing at the foot of my bed. They were dressed in white robes. They had no wings. I sensed that angels were surrounding my bed and my room didn't exist any more. The faces of the three in front of me were watching me intensely. Their eyes were watching me, guarding me, and the power I felt as they were doing this was incredible. Their faces were set like flint.

They were guarding my life from DEATH! In the upper right section of where my room had been was a dark presence, like a dark cloud-like something that I later realized was Death. I was aware of this, as if catching something out of the corner of my eye.

Behind the angels there seemed to be an excited commotion of "others" who were also present. I could almost hear whispering-like sounds, "others" who were excited and talking about me, others who had passed on. Died.

The angels were large, powerful looking, militant. They were on a mission. I tried to see who was there behind them, and I thought I saw two women. In my curiosity, I wanted to see who else was in the room.

Was it Mom? Was it Rose? They looked young. It was a hushed holy-like excitement and commotion, as if they were getting ready to see me.

Just thinking back as I write this all right now brings me to tears and goose bumps. It was all very awesome and so super REAL!

Now Is Your Time

No one said anything to me.

No one was touching me.

When I told my story to Fox News on Feburary 6, 2014, in San Antonio, Texas at the Methodist Texsan Hospital, the reporter stated it was the angels who had healed me. That's not what I said to him. I explained to him, as I am explaining now to you, that my encounter with my Healer and my bodyguards is my true account of my near death experience that I had.

Death wanted me, and they were there to stand guard so Death could NOT have me. It lasted merely seconds, but was tremendously powerful.

This brought me much courage and the CPAP became a little thing I just had to do. I had to do my part. I will never forget this vision, this gift of "seeing" I was given. It was a gift from my Father Yahweh.

He pulled back the veil, the curtain of this life, so I could see I was being well-guarded by divine beings and with that, I closed my eyes with supernatural peace and went to sleep.

And then the hands touched me again. I felt hands on my body in different places. Surely this time someone was in the room—the RN, the CNA, the respiratory tech—but no one was there!

"Father, You showed me the angels, but they were not touching me. Who's touching me? Please, tell me because this is weird!" And this is what He said to me.

"The people who want to be here in this room, cannot. But their prayers, like hands can be. Their prayers, like spiritual hands, are here, and they are laying their hands on you to bring you healing."

I wept.

My son and daughter wanted to be with me, others as well, but they were all so far away and loaded down with responsibilities, I could not expect them to come. Evidently, had I passed, they would have felt additional pain by not coming. Thankfully, they were spared. But their hearts, their hands, were reaching out to me and present in another way.

Their hands were reaching out to me to stay. Even now I think about my great-grandson, Bryce, in Becca's womb (my granddaughter), because I know she was praying for her DD, and he had to experience that. He was born April 2, 2014. He is the apple not only of his mother's eye, but everyone connected to him. What a darling!

It was an amazing moment to hear and understand

the power of prayer! My Father revealed to me what He wanted me to know very clearly. I could feel hands on my body. I knew many were praying — people who knew me and people who didn't. I will never forget those hands, nor the prayers of those who prayed for my life. Thank you. These two words seem so small. They can never express just how grateful, how thankful I am to be here, now!

Now, when I share my story, I am able to share with others how powerful prayer is and can be, especially, when we are miles apart from the ones we love and the ones we are praying for, those who are in desperate need.

Ask my niece Peggy Sue. Her fiancée, Anthony, was near death this year and he is alive! Thank you, Father, because we know you are the Divine Healer!!

We did get two visitors after that awesome night. As a surprise, my brother, Donald, and his wife Tammy walked into my ICU room with a gift bag in hand. I was so happy to see them I began to cry. It sure made my heart feel really good to see them. I love my family!

Now Is Your Time

A man once told us when you spell the word F-A-M-I-L-Y, it stands for:

- Forget
- About
- Me
- I
- Love
- You!

Remember? Yes, remember this, because when it comes to family, there's no one who can take their place, ever. Once they are gone, they are gone. Now is the time to love each other.

We spent several hours with Donald and Tammy. We laughed, joked, and just had a really sweet time. Donald and Tammy coming that day was so precious to us. I'll never forget that. They actually came back on January 2, 2014, the day I was discharged from the hospital, and they took us to their home in Killen, Texas.

CHAPTER 6

My Turning Point

Now Is Your Time

The hospital staff's hands at MTH were gentle, kind, caring, and healing. I became close with several of the staff while there. The entire staff was outstanding!

The mission statement of MTH is as follows:

> As part of the Methodist Healthcare family, our mission is serving humanity to honor God, and this philosophy is reflected in everything we do. We look forward to the opportunity to care for you and your family.

I can testify this mission statement is true!

We kept a list of the staff's names so we would not forget them or their service. We wanted to do something to show our appreciation because they (like the angels) took excellent care of us.

How can I honor them? A thank-you card is sweet, but I want them to feel honored, I thought to myself. Somehow, I would figure this out. We had their names. It was a growing list, a large list. If only I were rich, I thought as I prayed. These thoughts consumed me once I returned home, but we'll get to this a bit later.

Finally, I graduated from the ICU to a regular step-down unit on the second floor. I was so excited! It was New Year's Eve and my daughter's birthday. Soon I would be home in my own bed, and I was so happy. I missed everyone so much, especially my associates at the office. I had really missed being with them on the cruise.

The one person I missed the absolute most during my stay was my mother, Lucille (aka Lucy). When I think back thru all my years, my mom was the one who was always there for me. My heart yearned and ached for her physically. Somehow I knew she was aware of everything I was experiencing. She always said she had eyes in the back of her head. I believed her and I knew she was watching over me. I love you, Mom. I believe "many" were watching over me and still are.

Spending ten days in an ICU gives one a lot of time to think. I had hoped before the end of the year I would have a time to reflect over 2013. Well, I was certainly given my time without interruption! I realized some things I love realizing. Some things were revealed to me about my life I already knew, but I needed them to be revealed again. There were some new things as well. I love revelation. I believe self-examination is key and necessary in order to grow and learn. I realize being coachable only works in my favor. That NOTHING is ever a waste of my time when my intent is to love and be loved. And when I think I have wasted my life, I have learned to replace that thought with "No. I was learning, I was growing, I was seeking to succeed."

Now Is Your Time

I know now failing is part of the experience of life and makes one have more grit and determination to keep at it. If it's something we truly desire...we shall obtain it!

The question then becomes, how bad do we want it? I have discovered my WHY! When we know our WHY of what we want, then we shall have it!!

So what I desire to BE – DO – HAVE NOW becomes my focus, and it becomes a part of my WHY and my FOR WHO.

When we focus on what we WANT and take the action steps to receive it, it soon becomes our reality. Let's focus more on what we do want—love, joy, peace, success, health, wealth! And it's not just for ourselves, but for others.

This is my focus NOW.

Let's skip focusing on what we DON'T want because that is the OLD way, the OLD pattern. Why focus on the same old, same old as most do? We know the definition of insanity. "If we always focus on what we don't want, we will always continue to get what we don't want!"

What about YOU, my precious reader?

Now Is Your Time

What is it you think, feel, need, and want? When was the last time you had a good heart-to-heart with yourself? Sometimes, we NEED to be in time out! It's time we sat down with ourselves. It's time to get really clear. It's time to be very honest with ourselves and ask, "What's working and what's not?" If not now, when? If not, why not? We are the common denominator of every one of our life's situations. The responsibility for who I am is up to me. Who I am... who I am becoming...what I am achieving...what I am building...what legacy am I leaving...

YOU alone have the answer for YOU.

Why not spend the next twelve months focusing on being the BEST us, the best us we have ever been, and let's WATCH what happens! There will be changes, there will be transformation, and there will be measurable results. I have watched me each month during 2013. I am not the same.

The only person I can change is me. The only one who can change me is me. We are given FREE WILL. Have we forgotten this?

"If it's meant to be, it's up to me!" Right? Right! We do our part, we give it all we've got, we go until we can't go any further...WE CHOOSE how far that is.

How far do I want to go? I hear, "To the top! We won't

STOP till we're on TOP!" Great cheers! Great words! These help us take GREAT ACTIONS!

What are our gifts?

What are our talents?

Where are they? Are they being utilized daily? What are our dreams, our goals, our desires? What is our WHY?

I was revived and set on FIRE to get this message out!

The message of NOW!

NOW IS THE TIME is all about realizing it's our TURN...it's our TIME!

NOW! NOW! NOW!

It's never too late. You're never too old or too young to begin anything that your heart is on FIRE for!

GET FIRED UP!

I hope your flame has been fanned while you read my story to embrace your breath, your life, your wife, your husband, your children—everyone you know!

But just as importantly, embrace YOURSELF!!!

Now Is Your Time

This story is for you...it's for me...it's for everyone!

I already knew so many things about myself, but for me this entire ordeal had given me a new vision, a new reason for living, for being!

What was I doing with my life, with my gifts, and my talents? What was really going on? I had been given a second chance, and I knew I was not to squander it. Neither was I to keep my talents buried in the sand any longer. My focus was good. It was also divided. Once again my heart was all over the place. Listening to my HEART has been the place where my TURNING POINT began for me in 2014. It has been a new chapter and one I needed. We need all of our chapters.

What about you?

Are your gifts and talents hidden in the sand?

Are you in a hidden place, yet to be discovered?

Are your treasures buried deep within you? Is your life blooming?

Are you growing, or are you wilting on the vine of life? Are you?

I had been admitted with pneumonia. On discharge,

the doctor gave me a new diagnosis: acute interstitial pneumonitis. He wrote it down on a sheet of paper. In fact, he said he had recovered from it and I could, too, that he was an asthmatic and he had survived. I thought, "Well, if he can I can."

He told me he was sending me home on oxygen, and that I would have to sleep with it on at night. He said I'd have to carry a portable tank with me wherever I went. He told me to rest and stay away from people because my immune system was too low and to wear a mask whenever I was with people. He said the lungs take a long time to heal. Last thing he said was, "You'll need a specialist."

Acute interstitial pneumonitis is serious stuff! Once home, I researched it as soon as I could. Acute interstitial pneumonitis has no known cause and no known cure. In six months, you could die from it or have to have a lung transplant in order to survive it.

Joseph asked me why on earth I had looked that up. Well, I'm an RN—of course I was going to look up what the doctor had written down. Pneumonia was bad enough, but this discharge diagnosis was crazy scary. We chose to wait it out, and I am still here. HalleluYAH!

January 2, 2014, Donald and Tammy came to pick us up and we headed to their place. We spent the night.

Now Is Your Time

It was my first night without the hospital staff. I did okay. The next day Nathan and Starr (our niece and nephew from Kileen, Texas) drove us all the way to Dallas. We really love it here. It was a fun ride with these two young people. It was a day to rejoice, a day to get to know each other as adults. We had great conversations, we laughed and cried. We stopped at a restaurant we'd never eaten at before and had the most delicious Italian lunch.

Along the way, Starr shared with us that she wanted to get pregnant and was troubled she may not be able to conceive. Once home, after carrying up luggage to our third-story apartment, I was short of breath from climbing the stairs and my legs felt like jelly. I was still very weak. This near-death experience had taken a toll on my body. I got oxygen on me as soon as I could hook myself up. We thanked Starr and Nathan for bringing us home. We invited them to stay, but they had already taken a day off from work just to get us home. It was a turn-around trip of three and a half hours for them.

I asked if it was okay if we prayed for Starr. I had seen her tears, her desire for her own child. I felt it...we all did.

Before the kids left, we all laid hands on Starr's stomach. We agreed in prayer that certainly the Father could heal her within and that she would conceive a child. Nine months later, on October 1, 2014, Celeste was born! She was a beautiful baby girl born on her mother's birthday! You cannot get a better gift than that!

Prayer changes us, in this I am a firm believer. I believe everything that my Father Yahweh has shown me, and has spoken to me. He tells me:

I am who I AM says I am.

I am His and He is mine.

My destiny, my desire, is to BE all He desires for me to be, to do all He's planted in my heart to do and to have all He desires for me to have.

I believe Him.

I believe in the Be –Do – Have philosophy.

I knew very early in life He loved me. I have always loved Him.

I believe things happen for a reason. I believe in divine plans and purposes. I believe I was supposed to meet each one who touched my life with their literal hands.

Now Is Your Time

I not only wanted to shake their hands, but hug their necks. For the entire month of January 2014, a party was planned for the crew of Air-Medical and the staff of Methodist Texsan Hospital. The CEO of MTH (Marc and his crew) handled every detail. February 6, 2014 we got there early to see it all put together. There were certificates of appreciation with all the names we had collected. I know, because I signed them all! It was a beautiful party. Sometimes those who serve need honor and recognition for their services in BIGGER WAYS!

If our lives are not about serving through love, by loving, then why aren't they? To love and to be loved is the greatest gift of all! It is WHY we are here!

Our past paved the way for this day. Nothing is ever really lost, only a lesson that needs to be learned.

Be filled with love overflowing. Be that ever-burning fire of love, the real YOU! All you have is today.

Begin by loving, accepting, and cherishing yourself. You are one of a kind. Be the superstar that you are... the RED CARPET is before YOU. Own it! Call this your turning point!

NOW IS THE TIME! IT'S YOUR TURN!

IT'S YOUR TIME TO SHINE!

Chapter 7

This Is Not the End...

Only the Beginning

Now Is Your Time

Now Is Your Time

Let me begin by saying thank-you for reading my story. My story for *Now Is Your Time* began in 2000 with one thought. Actually it was a question. "If God had a watch, what would it look like?" I said to myself, "Well it wouldn't have numbers or hands, it would just say NOW." Thus, the message meant for me at the time was..."Now is the time."

This one inspirational thought that it was "now time" shifted me. It moved me to realize I needed to be about whatever I was doing because all I had was now. At the time, I had many dreams and goals: big ones, little ones, various ones. I still do. Because I love to write, I began journaling about everything. Journaling wasn't new because I wrote all the time. In fact, most of my journals, if you read them, are prayer journals about my goals, dreams, and wishes.

"Now is the time" has been the biggest and key motivating factor of pushing me up the proverbial hill of where I desire to go. One of our favorite pastors, Henry Wright, says it best. "It's a climb to the top, to the Holy Places. We take two steps forward and fall back one usually, but we're still progressing by one step." Staying positive has been the best decision of my life. One day at a time, one step at a time, and sometimes one great huge leap of faith is required.

I am leaping more and more. I invite you to begin

leaping too. Why not? If not now, when? We were born with a timer. It's called our heart. One day our timer, our clock, will stop. It will tick its last tock. What will we leave behind? Will we leave a legacy? How will our eulogy read? What will you be remembered for?

My hope and my prayer is this. That you knew me to be a loving, giving, sharing woman who deeply cared about you. That I made you laugh, I made you cry, that we had fun, we danced, we dined, that we had the best of times...that we both believed in the sweet by-and-by and that I'll catch you on the flip side. That life was meant to be shared and adored. That nothing is a waste of our time if the reason we are doing anything is because of love. That I loved you and saw how great and marvelous you truly are, like a bright shining star.

That "Now is your time" to soar and rise, to run, to trip and fall, and get up and go again and again!

And with that said, I leave you one last vision, image. Imagine, my friend, with me for just one moment. Think of me as I am thinking of you!

There she stands, right at the edge of the cliff. She looks up and the sky is bluer than ever, the sun beaming, the sunlight filling the earth, and peace filling her being. As she looks down into the sparkling blue river with the sunlight hitting it just right, it seems like diamonds laying there upon the waters. With one big, huge breath she leaps higher than she has ever leaped before, and off the cliff she goes...her heart filling with joy, her face radiant with happiness.

As she descends, seeing the water coming closer and closer, she spreads out her arms to their fullest extent. As she reaches the water, only her big toe feels its wet refreshing coolness, for an undercurrent of wind so powerful, more mighty than she has ever felt, picks her up to go higher. As her toe leaves the water, it creates just enough movement to leave a ripple effect, and she flies! She flies higher and higher, and oh, the view! She can see more than she has ever seen! Like an eagle, she flies. She is free, finally free, to soar and fly and to go so, so high. Her thoughts are amazing up there in the air—they are clear, crystal through and through. NOW she knows what she needs to do... write her story and tell you to write yours too.

With much love, happiness, and shalom peace, I'll see you at the top!

D'vora

NOW is YOUR time! Now go!

Now Is Your Time

About the Author

The eldest of eight children, D'vora Power was born to Donald and Lucille Power in New Orleans, Louisiana. As the eldest, there was much responsibility to be had in those days. There were no Pampers, no dishwashers, and everything was done by hand. Cleanliness was next to godliness and everything in their house sparkled.

Married to Joseph at a young age, D'vora and her husband have raised two children, are grandparents to seven, and great-grandparents to Bryce.

D'vora was a cosmetologist for twenty years, a registered nurse since 1993, and became a licensed massage therapist in 2006.

In 2013, she embarked on her newest venture as a financial wellness coach. D'vora is a speaker, author, teacher, and healer who loves to pray, have fun, and travel.

Now Is Your Time

Dreams Do Come True! It Can Happen to You!

D'vora Power educates single people and families on how to lower their taxes, get out of debt, and make their hard-earned dollars work harder for them. She teaches people how to save and invest in order to prosper. She recruits other like-minded people who want to achieve success.

In addition, she is a motivational speaker and author. D'vora is a member of the Public Speakers Association and has held several seminars on financial healing, realizing your dreams, and living life to the fullest.

You can reach D'vora at her office in Plano, Texas, or on her Facebook page at:

https://www.facebook.com/successwithdvora

101 East Park Blvd.
Suite 451
Plano, TX 75074
931-982-2226

www.ingramcontent.com/pod-product-compliance
Lightning Source LLC
Chambersburg PA
CBHW052116070526
44584CB00017B/2505